Who's Been Here?
A Tale in Tracks

Fran Hodgkins
Karel Hayes

Text copyright © 2008 by Fran Hodgkins
Illustrations copyright © 2008
by Karel Hayes
ISBN 978-0-89272-714-8

Library of Congress Cataloging-in-
Publication Data available on request

Printed in China

5   4   3   2   1

Down East
BOOKS·MAGAZINE·ONLINE
www.downeast.com

Distributed to the trade
by National Book Network

DEDICATIONS:

For Winston and Willy
—FH

To family and friends—
dog lovers all!
And a special thanks to
Lucy, Camryn, Aidan,
and of course Timber.
—KH

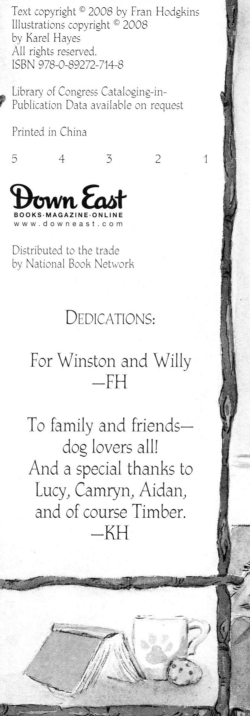

Willy loves the winter. He loves to run
around town and up into the woods.

There he goes! Willy! Wait for us!

Who's been here? Willy has. But who else?
These tracks are about half the size of Willy's
tracks. There are four toes.

A cat has been here.

Who's been here? Willy has.
But who else?

These tracks have only three toes, which point forward. They don't look like paw prints.

A turkey has been here.

Who's been here? These tracks look
a lot like Willy's, but they are smaller.

They have little claw marks above
each toe, just like Willy's.

A fox has been here.

Who's been here? Willy has. But who else?

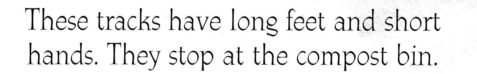

These tracks have long feet and short hands. They stop at the compost bin.

A raccoon has been here.

Who's been here? Willy has. And so has
someone else — someone with big feet and big strides.
Willy tried chasing this big-footed someone.

A rabbit has been here.

Who's been here? These tracks are not paw prints.
The have two halves. One set is much bigger than the other.

A deer has been here.

And so has a moose.

Who's been here?

Willy has. It looks like he didn't stay.
Those tracks are much bigger than Willy's.

A bear has been here.

Let's go back into town, like Willy did.

Who's been here? These tracks are small....

Do you smell something?

A skunk is here!

Willy! No!

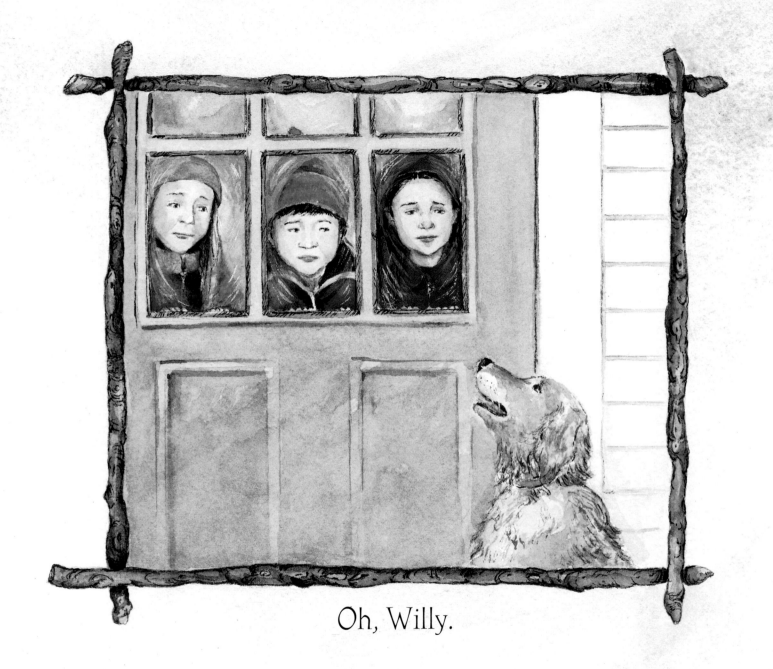

Oh, Willy.